little
scribe

PICK A PICTURE,

Write an Opinion!

by Kristen McCurry

CAPSTONE PRESS
a capstone imprint

A+ Books are published by Capstone Press,
1710 Roe Crest Drive, North Mankato, Minnesota 56003
www.capstonepub.com

For everyone at Minnewashta Elementary, a great school! —KM

Library of Congress Cataloging-in-Publication Data
McCurry, Kristen.
 Pick a picture, write an opinion! / by Kristen McCurry.
pages cm. — (A+ Books: Little Scribe)
 Audience: Ages 5-8
 Summary: "Introduces opinion writing to children using photographs as idea prompts"— Provided by publisher.
 ISBN 978-1-4765-4240-9 (library binding)
 ISBN 978-1-4765-5107-4 (paperback)
 ISBN 978-1-4765-5952-0 (eBook PDF)
1. Persuasion (Rhetoric)—Juvenile literature. 2. Authorship—Juvenile literature. 3. Photographs—Juvenile literature. I. Title.
 P301.5.P47M33 2014
 808—dc23   2013032325

Thanks to our adviser for her expertise, research, and advice:
Kelly Boswell, reading consultant and literacy specialist

Editorial Credits
Kristen Mohn, editor; Heidi Thompson, designer; Danielle Ceminsky, production specialist

Photo Credits
iStockphotos: Andrew Rich, 6-7, CREATISTA, 17, DenisZbukarev, 18, Okssi68, 8, Sadeugra, 28, Squaredpixels, 26-27, technotr, 26; Shutterstock: Algefoto, 11, Eldad Carin, 20-21, Galyna Andrushko, 12-13, Jamie Wilson, 1, Michael Zysman, 22, Okeanas, cover, Phil McDonald, 30, Rebecca Abell, 15, Trybex, 14, Zurijeta, 5, 25

Note to Parents, Teachers, and Librarians
This Little Scribe book uses full color photographs and a nonfiction format to introduce the concept of opinion pieces. *Pick a Picture, Write an Opinion!* is designed to be read aloud to a pre-reader or to be read independently by an early reader. Photographs help listeners and early readers understand the text and concepts discussed. The book encourages further learning by including the following sections: Table of Contents, Glossary, Read More, Critical Thinking Using the Common Core, and Internet Sites. Early readers may need assistance using these features.

Printed in the United States of America in North Mankato, Minnesota.
062016   009789R

Table of Contents

What Is an Opinion?

What is the best song? Who is the greatest sports star? How long should recess be? The answers to questions like these are opinions.

An opinion is the way someone feels or thinks about something. If you think summer is the best season, that's your opinion. Not everyone has to agree with an opinion. Someone else may like winter best.

Words and Pictures

Your opinion piece can include words and pictures. If you need help with your writing, ask your teacher.

An opinion piece or essay is writing that lets you share your opinion with others. You might just want to tell others what your opinion is. Or, you might want to try to persuade them to agree with you. The point you're trying to make is called your argument. Writing an opinion piece gives you a chance to make your feelings known.

Fact or Opinion?

Anyone could look at this photo and agree that the girls are dressed as superheroes. It's a fact. An opinion is different from a fact. It's something that people don't always agree on, such as which girl's outfit they like better.

Do you have an opinion about what the best super power would be? Ask your friends for their opinions.

The best topics for opinion pieces are ones that you feel strongly about or find interesting. Photos are a great way to get ideas for opinion pieces.

How to Begin

To start your opinion piece, use words like these:

- I like . . . I would like . . .

- I think . . . I feel . . . I believe . . .

- The best . . . The best thing about . . .

- My favorite . . .

- Everyone should . . .

- In my opinion . . .

7

Get to the Point

An opinion piece usually starts with the topic sentence. It lets people know right away what you're writing about and what you think about it.

On a sheet of paper, write these words and fill in the blanks with your opinions:

topic sentence

My favorite book is _____.
I like it because_____.

That's an opinion piece!

Reasons

In an opinion piece, you need to answer the question why. Why do you have that opinion? Giving reasons will help answer why.

For example, saying "red is my favorite color" won't help someone understand what you like about it. Maybe you like it because it's bright and cheerful. Or maybe it reminds you of your grandpa who's a firefighter. Detailed reasons will make your opinion piece stronger.

What is your favorite color? Why?

Who's Your Hero?

Do you have a hero? Maybe Abraham Lincoln, a famous athlete, a favorite teacher, or your parent is your hero. Write an opinion piece about a hero in your life. Be sure to tell why.

Make a List

Before you begin writing, make a list of reasons to support your opinion. Making a list will help you be sure that you have enough good reasons to write about. If you have trouble coming up with reasons for your topic, try another topic. Here's a list of reasons for an opinion piece on a hero:

- Uncle Pete is brave and kind.

- He served in the military.

- He helped me learn to ride a bike.

- He knows how to fix cars.

The Best Pet

What do you think the best pet is? Write about it. Or write about why you think you should be allowed to get a pet.

Find Out More

The more you know about your topic, the stronger your argument will be. If you'd like a snake as a pet, check out snake books from the library. Or visit a pet shop and ask questions about how to care for snakes. Then you can include strong reasons in your writing:

I would like a pet snake. I think I should be allowed to have one because I know how to feed them and how to keep their cages clean.

TV or No TV?

Kids and adults sometimes disagree about how much TV kids should watch. Write an opinion piece that explains your opinion about TV.

Use Linking Words

Linking words help move you from one idea to the next. Some examples are:

- because
- and
- also
- another
- other
- so

I think I should be allowed to watch TV for two hours each day <u>because</u> there are many good TV shows. Some TV shows teach me about science <u>and</u> nature. <u>Other</u> shows teach me about being a good friend. Some shows <u>also</u> make me laugh. <u>Another</u> reason I should be allowed to watch TV is <u>because</u> I will not bother my brother while I am watching. TV teaches me things <u>and</u> it keeps me out of trouble <u>so</u> I should be able to watch TV for two hours each day.

Should Kids Do Chores?

Most kids have strong opinions about doing chores. Do you do things at home to help out your family? What is your opinion about it? Should kids have to do chores?

Think About the Other Side

Keep in mind that others may not agree with your opinion. If your opinion is that kids should not have to do chores, do you think your parents would agree? Why or why not? Which of the following reasons do you think your parents would agree with more strongly?

- **Kids shouldn't do chores because they wouldn't have time left to watch TV.**

- **Kids shouldn't do chores because they wouldn't have time left for homework.**

You can make your argument more powerful by thinking carefully about which reasons you include.

A Reminder at the End

An opinion piece begins with a topic sentence and then lists reasons to support it. But how does it end? A good ending reminds readers of the main point. The conclusion to an opinion piece about picking up litter might be:

You can be a good citizen by picking up trash and keeping your city clean.

A Call to Action

In some opinion pieces, the conclusion is a call to action. It tells readers that if they agree with the opinion, they can do something to help, such as pick up trash or be kind to animals

Here's another topic. Do you think animals feel happiness? Write an opinion piece including a topic sentence, reasons, and a conclusion.

Animal for a Day

If you could be an animal for a day, which would be the most fun? Swinging like an ape? Flying like a bird? Write an opinion piece about your choice. Give strong reasons that will make your reader want to be that animal too!

Help from a Friend

Everyone has a bad day now and then. When you have a bad day, how do you like to be cheered up? Write an opinion piece about the best way to help a friend feel better.

Give Examples

Was there a time you helped a friend? If so, tell about it in your opinion piece. Sharing something you did or saw can be an example that will help support your opinion.

One time I gave my friend a hug after his dog died. He was still sad, but it made him feel better. You should let your friends know that you care about them.

Favorite Sport

Write an opinion piece about the sport you like best. If you don't like any sports, write about that instead.

Do you play on a team? Did your family go to a game? Did you get hurt on the field? Be sure to include examples that support your opinion.

Time for Bed!

Are you a night owl or an early bird? Write an opinion piece about what time you think your bedtime should be. Eight? Nine? Midnight? Don't forget to support your argument with reasons, including examples.

One time I stayed up late, and I wasn't even grumpy the next day.

Now you've got the hang of it! Opinion pieces can be a fun way to let others know how you feel. You can use opinion pieces to write about things you believe in or things you feel are fair or unfair. If you use good reasons, your writing might even persuade someone to agree with you.

Whether it's the best way to roast a marshmallow or the best flavor of ice cream, everyone has opinions. So let's hear yours!

Glossary

argument—an idea or opinion supported by reasons

chore—a job that has to be done regularly; washing dishes and taking out the garbage are chores

citizen—a member of a country or state who has the right to live there

conclusion—the last part of a piece of writing

detailed—full of description

essay—a piece of writing that gives the author's opinion on a particular subject

example—a model to be followed

persuade—to change a person's mind

reason—the basis or cause of a belief

support—to help something

topic—the subject of a piece of writing, talk, speech, or lesson

Read More

Fandel, Jennifer. *You Can Write a Terrific Opinion Piece*. You Can Write. Mankato, Minn.: Capstone Press, 2013.

Manushkin, Fran. *What Do You Think, Katie?: Writing an Opinion Piece with Katie Woo*. Katie Woo, Star Writer. North Mankato, Minn.: Picture Window Books, 2014.

Minden, Cecilia, and Kate Roth. *How to Write a Review*. Language Arts Explorer Junior. Ann Arbor, Mich.: Cherry Lake Pub., 2011.

Critical Thinking Using the Common Core

Read about topic sentences on page 9. Then turn to page 16 and read the sample opinion piece about watching TV. What is the topic sentence of that essay? (Key Ideas and Details)

Turn to page 15 and read the sample opinion piece about a pet snake. What two reasons does the author give to support the argument? What are some arguments you might use against having a pet snake? (Integration of Knowledge and Ideas)

The author says that even when we write opinions, we must support them with facts. Why is it important to support our opinions? Think of an opinion you have about an important topic. What facts could you use to support it? (Integration of Knowledge and Ideas)

Internet Sites

FactHound offers a safe, fun way to find Internet sites related to this book. All of the sites on FactHound have been researched by our staff.

Here's all you do:

Visit *www.facthound.com*

Type in this code: 9781476542409

Super-cool stuff!

Check out projects, games and lots more at
www.capstonekids.com